Focus.
Accomplish.
Grow.

The Business Owner's Guide to Growth

Andrew J. Birol

PACER associates ®

PACER Associates, Inc.
Solon, Ohio
www.pacerassociates.com

ひ

Printed in the United States of America.

Published by PACER Associates, Inc., Solon, Ohio, USA.
www.pacerassociates.com

ISBN 0-9707690-0-8

This book is dedicated to my daughter Margo,
who has taught me more about growth
than anyone else.

TABLE OF CONTENTS

This symbol which appears throughout the book, contains one of *Andy's Anecdotes,* useful and funny observations heard over the years.

FOREWORD

In an economy that's highly competitive, global, and knowledge-based, identifying, retaining, and nurturing the best customers is part art and part science. The "new economy" is here and in full swing, and it presents tremendous opportunities concealed amidst near-fatal risks for the entrepreneur.

Andy Birol has provided simple, focused, pragmatic techniques to avoid the traps and choose the right path. Drawing on his own entrepreneurial success as well as his decades-long assistance for small and mid-sized businesses, he provides the means to focus your business efforts on the highest potential opportunities while retaining the strengths that brought you this far. The glass is half-full and the remainder is all potential.

Over the past year, over 80 dot-com businesses have bitten the dust, including some with well-known brands, huge advertising campaigns, and apparently solid products and services. The rising tide of the economy does not lift all ships in these new seas. Growth is Andy's watchword, and he provides the template to pursue and exploit growth for businesses, profit centers, and sole practitioners. If you're an entrepreneur, Andy is your docent.

Andy maintains that growth is an attitude, that attitude determines behavior, and that behavior is, therefore, up to you. You can choose to be tossed by the winds and tides of competition, economy, technology, and the unforeseen, or you can plan to exploit the challenging changes that confront businesses today.

The Birol strategy is simple and straightforward. It is growth-oriented and constructively based. The separate articles are each self-contained templates for success in growth, profit, and harmony. Andy presents the simple steps in the science but, more importantly, is adept at the art.

Alan Weiss, Ph.D.
Author, "The Ultimate Consultant"

Dear Business Owner and Leader,

Growth–measured in terms of revenue and profit–may be stated in your business' goals. But, day-to-day, is it your company's passion?

In my 20 years of business experience and more now as a consultant, I have worked alongside hundreds of talented people. Many had great ideas and innovations. Others had numerous financial and operational resources. But too often, in spite of people, money and technology, their businesses fell short of their potential. Why? All these people, ideas, and company resources cannot be faulty.

Was the problem leadership? Not always. Many businesses have thrived without professional (or inspired) management. Something else was and is missing.

In these great economic times we tend to think we can have it all. But in the pursuit of seeking it all, too many companies don't accomplish what they must. Fortunes are lost, careers are impacted, and customers are disappointed. Looking back, it is often easy to see why. In my experience, most companies don't successfully grow for two reasons:

1. They do not choose among options.
2. They do not stay focused and committed.

This happens because companies over-complicate their lives. The immediate, urgent, and even critical can overwhelm any organization. So why not focus your company on growth as the simplest measure of staying on track? As long as growth can be profitable and does not come at the expense of customer satisfaction, growth can be the singular objective of any company.

I can almost hear you thinking...

"Yes, but, it is not that simple."
"Yes, but, our business is different."
"Yes, but, we don't look at the business in those terms."

My response is, why not try thinking about your challenges in terms of growth? If you do, growth:

• Is the proverbial "rising tide" that can lift many boats;
• Can conceal a great number of problems;
• Will create a future for your business.

In the pages that follow, you will find a consistent approach to problems faced by most companies. My goal is to simplify, focus, and resolve challenges in terms of growth. To me, this mindset resolves many questions, conflicts, and choices. Simply stated, when you have to make a strategic or a day-to-day decision, choose what will help your business to grow.

If you see the world as an abundant place and want to grow, you can grow.

It's a view of abundance, not scarcity.

It's a penchant for building, not just maintaining.

Growth is a state of mind. Enjoy all the clarity this will bring you and your company.

Andy Birol, *President*
PACER Associates, Inc.
www.pacerassociates.com

P.S. For a regular source of ideas on growth, subscribe to my free newsletter *Focus. Accomplish. Grow.* by going to www.pacerassociates.com

PART 1

Finding, Keeping, and Growing Customers

1

A METHOD TO THE MADNESS FOR BUSINESS-TO-BUSINESS COMPANIES

Your marketing team says the best way to increase sales is to buy new database marketing software. Or perhaps launch new distribution strategies. Or have salespeople make more cold calls. Or add telemarketing. What's the right answer?

Your customers feel neglected and don't do as much business with you as they used to. Your customer service manager recommends a "customer retention program." What should that program include? What channels should you use? Do you have the right software?

If you're in senior management, chances are these scenarios are painfully familiar. Decisions like these are crucial to your company's success. Is there a method to the madness?

The fact is, all marketing, sales, and customer service efforts come down to three basic goals: Finding customers, keeping customers and growing customers.

The technology advances in business have been incredible, but we've lost our focus. To get the greatest value from our efforts, we need to simplify our thinking and go back to the basics.

If you market products and services to businesses, ask yourself the following questions:

1. What is your company's best and highest use in the market-place? Are your products or services optimally bundled into a compelling offer?
2. Can you quickly identify the real pain that you resolve for custom-ers and explain how your product or service alleviates that pain?
3. Who are your very best customers? Targeted marketing requires a deep understanding of customers and their needs, which is gained only if you're exceptionally close to customers. *Have you asked your best customers why they like you, why they buy from you, and whether they'd refer you?* Referrals are an infallible measure of customer satisfaction.

The Crucial Intersection

If you can answer the three ques-tions above, you can identify the crucial intersection that should drive all your sales and marketing efforts. *It's the point where your firm's best offer is of most value to a narrow slice of the market because it resolves the greatest pain.* The more precisely you can define this intersection, the better you can pinpoint prospects. This should be the rallying point for all your company's marketing, sales, and customer service activities.

Using Sales Funnels to Guide Your Efforts

Defining your target prospect is the first step. Using a series of scoring tools that strictly adhere to your target prospect profile, you can create three sales funnels that will organize and imple-ment your plan for finding, keeping, and growing customers. All marketing, sales, and customer service activities must be designed, justified, and measured by their value to each funnel.

Finding Customers

The acquisition funnel systematizes the activities needed to turn suspects into prospects, prospects into qualified prospects, and qualified prospects into customers. Your goal of finding customers becomes the end and your marketing the means to the end.

The Acquisition Funnel

Keeping Customers

The retention funnel fulfills your goal of keeping customers, by progressively moving one-time buyers or ex-customers to the desired status of customers who make multiple or sustained purchases. These are the customers with the highest long-term value.

The Retention Funnel

Growing Customers

The development funnel is used to grow customers. Here the goal is to move stable customers through activities that convert them into up-sold or cross-sold customers and ultimately to the status of advocate or champion.

The Development Funnel

The results of these activities are obvious: a larger number of customers with the highest value to your company. The "graduates" of this three-funnel process are to be coveted and honored with no costs spared.

This system simplifies all your marketing, sales, and customer service activities. By returning to the basics – offer, need, and target market – you define your best prospects. This drives the creation, execution, and measurement of all sales and marketing activities through the acquisition, retention, and development funnels and provides a method to the madness.

On one hand, it's remarkably simple. On the other hand, your work has obviously just begun. Implementing and managing your business through this process requires discipline and passion. But when you have simple goals and clear paths to get there, the results are worth it.

Author's Note: For detailed steps on how to find, keep, and grow more customers, see Chapters 3, 4 and 5, respectively.

> **Sales, marketing and customer service activities can be tied to results and investments, but now who would want to do that?**

Andy has a web-based training program on this chapter.
To order this course, visit www.pacerassociates.com

2

WHEN MARKETING TO PROSPECTS, EXCHANGE INFORMATION OF VALUE!

If you sell a product or service to another business, you know it is critical to establish and maintain a meaningful dialogue with prospects. This is often expensive and can be awkward. But lessons can be learned from some of the better Internet web sites and from more traditional sources.

Consider the web-based jargon "permission marketing." After a prospect or other interested party has been successfully urged to visit a web site, they are asked to register their e-mail address to receive ongoing information of value. Hence the "e-term," *permission marketing*. Check out www.verticalnet.com, for a well-executed business-to-business example.

Before the Internet became popular, this process was known as exchanging information of value. A familiar example is the outbound telemarketer who calls to offer a free informational seminar or white paper in return for an executive's commitment of time and interest.

Regardless of the medium used to disseminate information of value, the process is the same:

1. Establish a dialogue with your audience.
2. Offer value.
3. Deliver what you promised.

This process can build better relationships. And, significantly, the right medium will also help you break through the clutter caused by information overload.

My own newsletter, _Focus. Accomplish. Grow._ is another example. Here are some interesting statistics from the effort:

- Fifty percent of the business cards in my rolodex/database already included an e-mail address. My assistant obtained e-mail addresses from another 35 percent. When contacted for an e-mail address, only one individual declined to provide it. That's a pretty good response and confirmed the importance of first establishing personal relationships and then maintaining them with technology.
- The effort involved in sending the newsletter is split between maintaining the e-mail addresses, writing and editing the issues, and producing the final mailing using Microsoft Word and Outlook.
- The biggest challenge is to provide the reader with a reasonable amount of useful information, but the feedback is very encouraging, and the value to my business has been high. The newsletter has resulted in a number of leads for consulting, speaking, writing, training, and testifying engagements.

Perhaps making an offer to exchange information of value would help your firm to _find, keep, and grow more customers._

3

ACQUIRING MINDS: FINDING CUSTOMERS EFFICIENTLY AND PROFITABLY IS A MATTER OF MASTERING THE ACQUISITION FUNNEL

When I ask business owners to choose their biggest sales challenge: Finding, keeping or growing customers, they always pick finding customers! Even though finding a customer is always harder than keeping an old one, nothing grows a business better than new business! But too often, a business' best intentions to acquire new customers fail. Why? Because they don't take a systematic approach to the challenge. They set unrealistic sales goals instead of preparing for success. Here are the key steps to find the customers you need.

1. Define your prospect's buying process.

Analyze how your prospective buyer will display interest, build desire, and take steps to do business with you. Clarify your understanding of a prospect's behavior until you understand it completely. Then, by examining your previous successes with your best customers, you will see a pattern emerge.

2. Outline your company's best way to close new customers.

From the time you initially target a prospect, exactly what happens as you move toward the close? Is there a single best way for your business to do this, or does it vary? When do you use direct mail, advertising, telemarketing, and face-to-face selling?

Identify the three most common sequences that result in closing an account. Once you have these scenarios down, take time to understand how you qualify your prospects. *Remember that time is valuable and all prospects are not created equal.*

3. Create definitions for your funnel.

With this wealth of raw data, it is time to bring structure to the picture. Using the funnel below, define each stage of the funnel for your business–from your suspect to your closed customer.

The Acquisition Funnel

- A **SUSPECT** is every company in your entire target market.
- A **PROSPECT** is an identifiable decision-maker in a company.
- A **QUALIFIED PROSPECT** is a decision-maker who has the time, need *and* the authority, and money to pay for your product or service.
- A **DEVELOPED PROSPECT** is someone you send a proposal, quote or sample.

Suspects
Prospects
Qualified Prospects
Developed
Closed

4. Determine how many new prospects you need at each step of the funnel.

To start, divide your average sale from a first-time buyer into your new customer sales goal. This gives you the number of first-time buyers you must land.

Then, move up the funnel and decide how many prospects you need at each step. If you need to qualify 10 prospects for each buyer you close, then plan to do so. Similarly, if you need to contact 1,000 suspects to identify a qualified prospect, then identify enough names and dedicate adequate resources to do so.

5. Understand what your prospects are worth and what you can spend to get them.

Now that you know how many new customers you need to meet your goal, determine what each prospect is worth to you.

- Divide the number of prospects it takes to close a sale into the value of the sale. For example, if a sale is worth $1,000 and you need 10 prospects to close one sale, then a prospect generates $100 of revenue.
- If you must spend $100 to create those 10 prospects, then each prospect costs $10.
- By subtracting the cost of a prospect, $10, from the revenue of a prospect, $100, you have $90, the real value of a prospect.

This exercise is critical as it gives you a benchmark of what to invest in a prospect and what to expect in return. *You now have a budget and confidence to spend just enough to obtain your new customers.*

6. Find great new customers effectively.

With financial guidelines in place for finding new customers, it's time to choose your tactics. Determine your sales, marketing, and customer service activities for each step of the funnel.

You may want to use face-to-face sales to close business, but may choose to emphasize direct mail over telemarketing or advertising to qualify prospects. Evaluate your activities, tools, and programs based on how cost-effective they are in terms of delivering the number of prospects you need.

Your choices will be easier and less risky because they will be based on meeting goals you have set.

Remember, finding customers efficiently and profitably is easier if you:

- Focus on your goal of *converting prospects,* not creating sales and marketing programs;
- Monitor both the quality and quantity of the prospects you process through your sales funnel;
- Continually evaluate your efforts to find new prospects, to ensure they're paying off.

> Finding customers is like dating. Don't expect a commitment until you have built a relationship.

Andy has a web-based training program on this chapter.
To order this course, visit www.pacerassociates.com

4

KEEP THEM COMING BACK: MAXIMIZING YOUR COMPANY'S CUSTOMER RETENTION AND PROFITS IN ONLY SIX STEPS

K eeping customers is a key success factor for any business. The actual value of a business is often determined by future cash flow from existing customers. And of course, cash flow provides the financing for the investment in finding new customers and for most other needs of the business.

To meet your company's goals, you probably have a mental picture of what activities and processes will maximize customer retention and profits. And if you believe there is a "right way" for your business to retain customers, why not define your best practices just as you would for accounting or manufacturing?

Here are six easy steps to lead your customers through the retention sales funnel:

1. Define your new buyer's "bonding process."

Determine how your new buyer will gain confidence, recognize value, and build a continuing relationship with your business. That will help you clarify your understanding of your buyer's behavior. Then, by examining your previous successes with first-time buyers whom later became great customers, you will recognize a pattern.

2. Outline your company's best way for keeping customers.

From the moment you land a first-time buyer, exactly what do you do as you attempt to retain him or her? When do you use customer service, sales, telemarketing, and the Internet? Is there a best way for your business to do this, or are customer service functions handled randomly? Try to identify the three most likely sequences that result in keeping customers.

3. Create definitions for your funnel.

With this wealth of raw data, it is time to bring some structure to the picture. Using the funnel below, define each stage of the funnel for your business, from your one-time buyer to your reorder buyer.

Typically a **one-time buyer** is someone who is testing a larger relationship with your business. You have offered, or they have selected, a single product or service that allows them a low-risk method for sampling your firm and its capability to deliver on its promises.

The Retention Funnel

One-time Buyer / Win Back

Reordering Buyer

Customer

A **win-back buyer** is similar to a one-time buyer, although they have a previous, probably negative, experience with your firm. Often these "damaged" buyers, if "repaired," are the best candidates for becoming stable customers.

A **reorder buyer** is someone who has made a passive decision to repeat his or her initial decision to work with you. They may not have had a great initial experience, but their expectations were met. While they are not yet loyal, they see potential for this.

4. Determine how many new buyers you need at each step of the funnel.

To start, divide your average sale from a stable customer into your sales goal from retained customers. This gives you the number of stable customers you must land. Then move up the funnel and decide how many buyers you must attract at each step. If you need to qualify two reordering customers for each kept customer you create, then plan to do so.

5. Understand what your customers are worth and what you can spend to get them.

Now that you know how many customers you need to meet your goal, decide what your one-time buyers are worth to you:

- Divide the number of one-time buyers it takes to create a stable customer into the value of a stable customer. For example, if a stable customer sale is worth $4,000 and you need four first-time buyers to create a stable customer, then a first time buyer generates $1,000 of revenue.
- If you must spend $100 to create those four one-time buyers, then each prospect costs $25.
- By subtracting the cost of a first-time buyer, $25, from the revenue of a prospect, $1,000, you have $975, the real value of a prospect.

This exercise is critical as it gives you a benchmark of what to invest in a first-time buyer and what to expect in return. Don't over-deliver on service. Instead, set and agree on a level of service and provide what is expected. If you follow this rule of thumb, you will now have a budget and confidence to spend just enough to obtain your stable customers and maximize your profits.

6. Create stable customers effectively.

With financial guidelines for keeping customers in place, it's time to choose your tactics. Pick your sales, marketing, and customer service activities for each step of the retention funnel. For example, you may want to use seminars to create stable customers, but may choose to emphasize customer service over sales reps to create reordering customers. You can evaluate your activities, tools, and programs based on how cost-effectively they deliver the number of stable customers you need. Your choices will be easier and less risky than ever, because they will be based on meeting goals you have set.

> Set expectations, agree on expectations and meet expectations to create stable customer relationships.

Andy has a web-based training program on this chapter.
To order this course, visit www.pacerassociates.com

5

SIX STEPS TO GROW YOUR CUSTOMERS

If your business retains stable, profitable customers, definitely consider turning them into advocates and champions for your products and services. It's easier than you may realize to get your best customers to help you promote your business to prospects, but it requires a careful blend of technical, financial, and relationship skills.

1. Define the "bonding process" for turning your best customers into advocates and champions.

How do your better customers adapt your products and services to best suit their individual needs? *Do those customer relationships resemble partnerships or strategic alliances? If so, these are your potential champions.* They can help by introducing your firm to prospects. Once you determine how these customers become champions for your business, a pattern will emerge that you can duplicate.

2. Outline your company's process for growing advocates and champions.

When you land a customer, plot the development of the relationship. Is there a particular point where you begin to involve them in your new product development process or customer councils? If so, what led to this point?

Is there a best way for your business to get to this point, or does it seemingly develop at random? Try to identify the three most likely sequences that result in growing champions. But remember: *Companies do not become your champions or advocates, the people in them do.*

3. Create definitions for your development from customer to champion.

Determine each stage of the process–from a closed customer to an advocate or champion. Typically, a stable customer has hit some milestone in his or her relationship with your business. It could be a third purchase, the purchase of a service that increases dependency, or the exchange of previously withheld information or advice. Pinpoint these milestones.

At this point, a buyer evolves into a customer. Then look for when the customer begins to buy multiple products and services. It's around this time when they may ask to participate in customer councils, suggest strategic alliances, or want to test pilot new products and services. That is when the customer becomes a cross-sold or up-sold customer, and it's a good sign he or she is well on the way to becoming a champion.

Customers take the final step and become champions when they give you a reference and provide ongoing referrals. It means they believe in you and your firm and will proactively help you succeed.

4. Determine how many champions and customers you need at each step of the development cycle.

Divide your average sale from a customer into the total sales you expect from your advocates. This gives you the number of advocates you must land. Decide how many customers you need at each step. If you need to qualify three cross-sold or up-sold customers for each advocate you cultivate, then plan to do so. Similarly, if you need to land five customers to produce three cross-sold or up-sold buyers, then land enough customers and dedicate the resources to do the job.

5. Understand what your champions are worth and what you can spend to get them.

Too many customer relationships whither from inattention,

another form of under-spending. Here is a three-step method to ensure that doesn't happen.

- Divide the number of customers it takes to create a champion into the revenue of a champion. If you need five customers to create a champion and a champion generates $50,000 of revenue, then a customer represents $10,000 of potential champion revenue.
- If you decide you must spend $5,000 to create a champion, you can spend up to $1,000 cultivating each customer.
- By subtracting the cost of developing five customers, $5,000, from the revenue of a champion, $50,000, you have $45,000, the real value of a champion.

This exercise is critical because it provides a benchmark of what to invest in a champion and what to expect in return. Often, the investment will not be a direct cash outlay, but rather one of staff time and expertise.

6. Create champions effectively.

With the financial guidelines for keeping champions in place, choose your tactics. Pick your sales, marketing, and customer service activities for each step of the customer development. You may want to use seminars to cross-sell or up-sell customers, but may choose to emphasize executive tours and referral kits over more sales rep visits to create champions.

> "If you know your customers better, it is amazing what else they might buy from you."

Evaluate your activities, tools, and programs based on how cost-effectively they deliver the number of champions and advocates you need. Your choices will be easier, because they will be based on meeting your goals you have set.

If you focus on your goal of creating champions, you will have the ultimate benchmark for delivering excellent customer service. This is because a satisfied customer will refer your firm to prospects, while an unsatisfied customer won't.

Andy has a web-based training program on this chapter.
To order this course, visit www.pacerassociates.com

6

ASSESS CORPORATE CULTURE WHEN CHOOSING YOUR NEXT CUSTOMER

It's standard practice to qualify a prospect on the basis of time, need, authority and money, but why not by corporate culture as well? We all find it easier to work with some companies just as we prefer working with some employees more than others. In fact, as a result of outsourcing, with more and more work going to suppliers instead of employees, perhaps the supplier-customer relationship should (and will) start to mimic the employee-employer relationship.

If this is so, then as suppliers, we should start to assess our prospect's corporate culture just as we did when deciding to accept a company's job offer. While I'm not recommending pre-relationship psychological testing, we may need to run a relationship check just as we would a credit check. Since people still buy from people (as opposed to companies), some level of compatibility is essential. After all, customer-supplier relationships fail most often because expectations were not set, agreed upon, and then met. Some relationships may be already doomed from the start!

So let's take a few moments and decide whether we are picking good long-term partners or "one-time sales stands."

- Does the decision-maker communicate like you do?
- Does he/she share some basic values with you?
- Does his/her company make decisions like yours does?
- How are disputes resolved, or, *are* they are resolved?
- Is it a conservative or progressive environment in terms of risk-taking, communication, problem solving, and partnering?

While sales goals have to be met, they are rarely accomplished through the first order. Therefore, developing an ideal customer profile before closing that first deal will help ensure that more will follow. Taking a few minutes when moving qualified prospects through the developed or proposal funnel stage prior to closing them will only enhance the chances of successful long-term partnerships. This profile can easily be added as part of your qualifying customer or pre-proposal questionnaire.

It used to be said that if you want to know how a company treats its employees, look at how it treats its vendors. Today, the opposite holds just as true!

> When choosing between ego and greed, work with those motivated by greed. They will be more likely to change.

7

SPEND SMART TO GROW YOUR BUSINESS

While it's true that sometimes you need to spend money to make money, smart businesses understand that funds devoted to attracting customers must stand up to the same scrutiny as any other investment made by the firm.

Here's the single most important rule to remember: *Invest enough to breakeven on the customer's first order, and only close the type of customers you will profit from over time.*

Software companies and equipment lessors are examples of businesses that price their products low enough to easily attract new customers, but with the mechanisms in place that allow them to profit substantially over time. When implementing the "breakeven rule," remember: *All new customers must exhibit the potential to add value to your top and bottom lines.*

Customer relationships are built by consistently adding value over the long term. The right kind of customers *will* be profitable.

> If you want something done right, give it to the busiest company or person you can find.

8

THE MYTH OF THE TOTAL SOLUTION PROVIDER

In an otherwise forgettable movie named *Return to Eden*, Rosie O'Donnell plays an undercover detective being pursued by an amorous young admirer. At one point he pleads, "Just tell me what you want, I can do everything for you." To this O'Donnell replies, "If you really want to please me, go paint my house!"

How many times have we been pursued by sales reps and marketing campaigns stating they have the total solution for us? And when has a total solution been what we really needed? Too often, businesses assume their prospects want it all at once. Here are some common examples of total solution providers pushing their whole product line at the same time.

- Telecommunications companies that offer phone, cellular, e-mail, pager, and voice mail services.
- Banks that advertise checking, credit card, investments, and mortgages.
- Internet service companies that promote strategy, design, hosting, and fulfillment services.

The Fatal Flaw of Offering Everything

Besides the fact that it is very difficult to present many products all at once, it usually doesn't work for the customer either. Here are three reasons why.

- Customers want to test a company's ability to deliver one product at a time. In other words, they want to date before going steady.
- Customers have specific needs. There is almost always a product or service they would choose to try before others.
- If forced "to take it all or leave it," a customer may buy a total solution. But at the first sign of disappointment, the customer's remorse will overflow.

Does this mean that it is foolish to offer customers a variety of products to meet their individual needs? No. Instead, first take these three steps for selling customers all you can.

Three Steps:
1. Understand your customers' typical buying patterns.
2. Offer your products and services in the right order for your customers.
3. Market your products and services in the right order for your customers.

A. Understand your customers' typical buying patterns

Analyze what your customers buy from you. Determine which products or services are:

- The first ones they buy.
- The ones that encourage return purchases.
- The impulse purchases that don't lead to more.
- The ones that existing customers buy.

Here is an example of the above four products we can all relate to—Telephone companies promote:

- Long distance deals to attract first time buyers.
- "Friends and family" deals to lock them into a long term relationship.
- Telephone equipment as impulse purchases.
- Personal 800 numbers to existing customers.

B. *Offer your products and services in the right order for your customers.*

Sequence and stage your products and services and offers:
- Conversion products which convert prospects into first time buyers.
- Reorder products which prompt first time buyers to become regular customers.
- Next logical products which cause first time buyers to expand their relationships with a vendor.

When I served as a Product Manager for the Bank of Boston, we:
- Offered CDs to attract prospects with funds to invest.
- Created rollover programs to encourage CD customers to reorder our product.
- Advertised checking products to build long term relationships with CD buyers.

C. *Market your products and services in the right order for your customers.*

Create sales and marketing programs that offer products and services in the correct order and to prospects and customers who are ready to buy them. Here are some recent examples from the news:
- Sprint Telecommunications offered a telephone hotline pre-selling Rolling Stones tickets to anyone willing to switch over their long distance.
- Progressive Insurance does a magnificent job of telling its less attractive customers that their policies would cost less if they switched to the competition.
- Amazon.com provides topical newsletters to customers based on their previous purchase history, correctly assuming they can be up-sold or cross-sold.

In conclusion, it is possible to offer a wide range of products and services to customers without overwhelming them. The effort must be organized and presented in a systematic process based on how and when customers buy. Do not try to sell products and services on your schedule! Rather, understand your customers' behavior and adapt your company's approach accordingly. In other words, perhaps Rosie O'Donnell's overzealous admirer should have taken her advice and first painted her house!

> **If a company has never failed, they have never set their own goals high enough.**

PART 2

Growing Your Business in the New Economy

1

LESSONS FROM THE BLEEDING EDGE: SIX STEPS TO ENHANCE YOUR ONLINE BUSINESS SUCCESS

You run a healthy business and have built a consistent track record, but your company still isn't enjoying the benefits of being online. As a small business owner managing online efforts and a consultant to clients with web strategies, here are some important lessons I have learned.

In the past several years, hundreds of thousands of businesses in virtually every industry have launched web sites. Their "webmasters" promised increased sales, more leads, and reduced promotional costs.

In spite of the considerable resources devoted to these online investments, the rewards did not materialize. Sales did not skyrocket, few qualified leads were produced, and promotional costs (associated with maintaining the site) went up, not down.

What went wrong? In my experience, the most common mistakes start with six seemingly innocent statements.

The Six Mistakes:

1. *"I can be just like Mike."*
   –Don't assume your smaller, local or regional business can build even a proportional level of Internet awareness, transaction, or credibility compared to that of larger firms.

2. *"If I spend money, I'll make money."*
   –Don't be convinced that spending large sums building and promoting your web site will automatically yield results.

3. *"Business on the Internet is different."*
   –If your business is not successful off-line, it probably won't succeed online.

4. *"My web page is my online strategy."*
   –A web site is not an online business.

5. *"Everyone likes visiting my web site, just look at all the free information I give away."*
   –Providing valuable information doesn't ensure return visits to your site.

6. *"Of course I have a web strategy, look at all I have invested in graphics and technology."*
   –A clear business plan is needed and it has nothing to do with graphics or technology.

A common thread emerges through all six mistakes. We all must reconcile that we have learned on the Internet with our years of business sense and experience.

> When interviewing anyone for anything, find out if they: can do the job, will do the job, and how will they do the job.

A Guiding Principle for Future Online Success:

"With a plan, the Internet can help me to better reach, sell, and help all those who are or should be connected to my business."

With this mantra in place, here are six steps to make the Internet work for your business:

1. Identify your business constituents. Make a list of all the suppliers, employees, prospects, customers, and partners in your business world.
2. Determine the kind of valuable, current information each constituent needs from you.
3. Identify where they currently get the information and from whom.
4. Determine how good their current information is. Ask them if it meets their needs.
5. Decide how the Internet can improve and expand on this information, making your site "sticky." Learn which competitors have successful on line businesses and how they continuously provide and deliver this information to their constituents.
6. Create an e-business strategy based on exchanging information of value with your constituents. Decide which of your business objectives can be met online and how you will do it.

The basics of effectively communicating with your constituents hold as true online as they do in a traditional setting. The Internet can be far more than an electronic brochure for your business, but it is also far less than a new solution to off-line problems.

Start your e-strategy today by understanding what you need to say and who needs to hear it, and determine your return on investment in doing this. Only then does hiring Internet technologists and designers make sense. What doesn't make sense is hiring them before you come to the right conclusions.

You wouldn't delegate responsibility to outsiders for signing your checks, so don't leave strategic decisions to others either. This is both good traditional–and Internet–business sense.

2

ALLIANCES: KEY TO GROWTH
IN THE NEW ECONOMY

As small business owners, we need to generate awareness on shoestring budgets, and many of us wonder if the Internet is the key to growing our bottom line.

At the dawn of the Internet age, the pioneers among us hoped an online presence would translate into big business. Optimistically, we built web sites and registered with the top search engines. But quickly we learned that the Internet doesn't level the playing field for small businesses as much as the pundits preached. Then the experts confirmed our worst fears. Their solution for building awareness took on a painfully familiar sound, "You need to spend money to make money."

They advised us to invest in expensive banner ads and space on popular web sites; create a direct-mail, print, radio or television campaign in conjunction with our online presence; and stick "dotcom" at the end of our company's name–in the hope that a venture capitalist would discover our firm and help us eventually cash in with IPO gold.

Personally, that advice leaves me feeling that the more things change, the more they stay the same. But before the Internet dream fades away, let me suggest reasons to stay optimistic.

The Internet is entering a new phase of development in the new economy. *Pure Internet companies have learned that customers want traditional, off-line services just as much as they want the convenience of the Internet.* There's a name for this trend of combining online and off-line business. It's called "bricks and clicks."

To gain more visibility for our small businesses through the Internet, we should build on our traditional strengths, combining them with those we are gaining in the new economy.

The small business has always thrived by being nimble and responsive. Remember the strategies that work, particularly networking and referrals. Your good work speaks for itself.

Through the new economy, access to information, suppliers and buyers is changing radically. Small businesses have a few advantages:

- What you know is valuable. Small businesses can provide bite-sized information on the Internet to showcase their knowledge and skills.
- The Internet allows you to have essential personal conversations with prospects, referral sources, and networking groups. These conversations are highly worthwhile.
- Larger companies are growing more dependent on smaller companies to help meet their needs. The Internet provides access to services that big companies formerly managed internally.

If one of your key business needs is building awareness, develop Internet alliances. Alliances build on your traditional strengths while leveraging the new economy.

There are four key areas for building alliances. Each offers you opportunities to be heard by a larger audience. Make sure to explore your role in offering the following:

1. **Content.** What information of value does your business have that prospects, referral sources, and networkers need? Consider hosting articles, newsletters, and training on your site to offer additional value.
2. **Technology.** Work with firms that enhance your knowledge and wisdom through their technology. For example, I work with www.fancemail.com to deliver my newsletter in a user-friendly manner.

3. **Awareness.** Get listed and quoted on every relevant web site in your customers' industries.
4. **e-commerce.** Join every electronic business exchange you can find. Many are in their infancy, and most are free.

Building relationships is an essential ingredient in growing your business online and off-line. The only barrier to a small company's participation in the new economy is lack of confidence in trying new approaches. Learn to do this by building new alliances, experiences, and knowledge.

Never barter for anything you haven't already chosen to buy.

3

GROWING YOUR BUSINESS AND GOING ONLINE: SIX HARD LESSONS

H opes and budgets have been raised and lowered as firms experimented with the Internet, hoping it could help grow their businesses. What was learned? And as the Internet moves past its commercial infancy and into business "toddler" status, what can it do to help our businesses now?

While there are many benefits to the Internet, the focus here is on connecting the growth of your business to the proven capabilities of the Internet. To do this, let's assume that growing your business means:

- Creating valuable products and services.
- Getting more customers and prospects.
- Delivering what you offer.
- Profiting and growing.

If growing your business means doing these things, then there are some clear lessons to learn. Here is what has and has not worked to date.

When going online, **sell what sells**

Buyers buy products and services they already know. If your product offerings are the same–off and online–existing buyers will buy from your web site. Consumer and business sites like Dell, Staples and Charles Schwab all enjoy healthy sales from existing customers, who are comfortable buying the same products in a more convenient matter. If your buyers know your products or services well, then sell them online. Don't expect your web site to create brand awareness.

Buyers are buying from companies they already trust: Your online image is your off-line image. Disney, Continental and IBM can immediately sell their products online. If your company's image is positive, your loyal customers will go online to buy. Otherwise it is an uphill battle. While the web will reinforce your company's image, it will not create a presence that wasn't already there.

Sell real things from real companies.

"*A channel is not a business*," says Mohan Sawhney, a noted Internet theorist. If an Internet business is only a storefront for another company's products and services, it may not be a business. Just as off-line distributors are struggling to add value, so are Internet intermediaries. Any middleman must offer favorable packaging, service, value, warranty or terms. Otherwise consumers will go to the source to buy. It just seems safer. This helps explain the downturn of www.etoys.com, and even, potentially www.amazon.com.

A product line is not a company. Few stand-alone products have survived as online companies because businesses and consumers want to buy from an organization. This is because most people prefer browsing a brand name site like www.steelcase.com instead of www.officechairs.com. An online store for a single product line may not last long. Visiting these sites can feel like watching a late night TV commercial selling a greatest hits CD of an aging musician. You might buy from them once on a whim, but probably not come back. Feature your company. Don't be the next one-hit wonder.

Don't expect sales from strangers.

If you build it, they will not come. Few companies can create an online market for their products and services. Without millions of dollars in promotion, your business will not become the next www.ameritrade.com. Web sites are not billboards along a highway; they are mailboxes on cul de sacs. Not many people will find your site without first knowing about your company. These days, search engines return 10,000 or more responses to a query. How likely is it that your business will get a random call from an interested party? Probably not often enough to cover the investment in a great web site.

If you sell through a portal, you have given away your control. Just as with an independent distributor, wholesaler or rep group, selling your product or service on another company's web site has its perils. Do you get to know who your buyers are? What are they buying? What are they paying? How is your product positioned next to your competitors? Make sure your product or service is presented and sold as you intended.

Sell your differences, or sell to everyone.

Provide information that makes your company invaluably unique. Take a look at www.gettyone.com/en-us/home/home.asp. They provide an easy way to buy stock photos. How can you combine your company's products, services, and expertise to really stand out? If you succeed, then others cannot copy you. This is critical because on the Internet your competitors can copy your site overnight.

Run with the big dogs if you can. If your product is truly a commodity, and you have the lowest costs in the business, then exploit the Internet for all you can. Join every selling service, auction house, and vertical market you can find. Sites like www.freemarkets.com can help you expand your customer base. These sites will let you push prices down to your marginal costs and gain market share. If you can, squeeze your competitor's margins until they quit. You may laugh all the way to the bank.

Sell it now or fuggedaboutit!

Set six-month goals for your firm's online sales and costs. Define how your site will help your company grow. Will it improve sales, leads, fulfillment or image? Assume you will overhaul your site every six months. This will focus your organization on making your web site pay off as soon as possible.

There is no long-term payback, only more investment to keep up. A web site is like a child. Bringing it into the world is only a fraction of what it will cost to raise it into maturity. Plan for recurring maintenance, complete overhauls, and one huge mistake along the way.

If you can't sell, serve.

Provide value. If it is clear you cannot profitably sell your product or service online, then don't try. Instead, make your web site a must-visit site for your prospects and buyers. Provide value, knowledge, service, and other expertise and experience that will help your marketplace succeed.

Link into a community. If you cannot attract enough traffic to cost-justify more than a small web presence, then sell, trade or donate your company's expertise to other Internet locations that can showcase your value. Register with all the communities and content providers you can. Write, chat, join, and deliver as much as possible to people in your target market.

Will the internet help my business grow?

For a traditional (non- "dot-com") business, the answer is probably not much in the short run. For most companies, the excitement of launching a web presence is being replaced with a realization that the Internet is good at leveraging a firm's strengths and exposing its shortcomings. In fact, the Internet does this faster than any other marketing, sales, or customer service effort.

So, addressing the core issues of how a company can grow is still critical. To review, a company must:

- Create valuable products and services.
- Get more customers and prospects.
- Deliver what it offers.
- Profit and grow.

Where does your company stand? For many companies, the Internet has exposed the need to focus on the core issues of growth. If you figure out how your company needs to grow, you can then use the Internet to your advantage.

> When actual results don't measure up to ambitious plans, it was probably testosterone talking.

4

TEN REASONS
TO GO BACK ONLINE

I was speaking recently at an e-commerce seminar with Tom Zych of Thompson, Hine and Flory on the topic of why businesses should continue to throw resources at the Internet despite the dubious returns most businesses are experiencing. One of the topics we had the most fun with was that in spite of the "Great Internet Shakeout," why would an intelligent business owner continue to throw good money after bad into their e-strategy. Well, here are 10 good reasons to stay focused on your company's e-strategy.

10. The medium is established.
Web traffic continues to increase as do the number of web site visits and e-commerce.

9. There is no variable cost of distribution.
The Internet provides the ability to communicate with a million people as cheaply as one person. So with no variable distribution cost, the net cost to reach those people becomes zero.

8. It turns technology into relationships.
Few technologies really humanize communication the way the Internet does. You can truly express who you are and what you are to somebody online.

7. **It helps you turn relationships into value.**
   The Internet allows a visitor to indicate preferences, interests, and opinions, which form the basis for interaction, and thus a relationship. And in business, it's all about relationships.

6. **Pornographers are never wrong and they're never broke.**
   The videotape, video store and, quite frankly, VCRs all owe their early success to the pornography industry. While a distasteful role model, it's important to recognize success when you see it: 60 percent of Internet commerce is still pornography-based.

5. **Leverage, leverage, leverage.**
   In the era of knowledge businesses, what we know is often all that we are worth. Therefore, take your knowledge and leverage it online. Your articles, experiences, case studies, and client studies are more interesting than you may think. Inventory them and make them easily accessible examples of your business.

4. **It makes us them and them us.**
   As Paul Simon says, "One man's ceiling is another man's floor." Your different roles of vendor, customer, peer, and competitor can all be fleshed out and communicated to those who need to see you in those terms. This way, you can simultaneously extend all your critical relationships.

3. **You either have inventory or information.**
   Long before the buzz word "supply chain" came into vogue, it was clear American distribution channels were contracting. The Internet gives you two choices—either convey information or carry inventory.

2. **Your suppliers are online.**
   Think of everything your firm buys. How much of it do you—and could you—buy online? Chances are, most of what you need is waiting for you there. If your vendors are there, you should be too.

1. **Your customers are online.**
    How many of your customers are doing business online? If a majority are selling online, how often do they stay online and look for vendors. Are you at risk by not being there? Even though commerce may not be occurring online, impressions and preferences are being reinforced and revised daily.

    Going back online is not too different from your plans for the weekend following the first party you went to in college. You swear you will exercise better judgment, but you have no intention of staying home. As the weekend beckons, so does e-commerce. The key is to play the game intelligently and with greater forethought.

Fail fast and fail forward.

5

GOOD IDEAS DON'T NEED ANGELS

Recently I have read or overheard several discussions on "angel investors" and why there are not enough of them. This discussion usually turns into the lament of why high tech and Internet businesses have such a tough time getting started.

Ever since the "dot-com" crash, more and more bootstrap, kitchen-table entrepreneurs are turning to "angel investors" as their best source of financing. The rationale is that since the angel was once a struggling young lion himself, he or she should have a more lenient financial heart than that of a venture capitalist or banker. And with the return to sobriety among professional investors in "dot-com" and other high tech companies, it is true that the purse strings of the mainstream financial sources have significantly tightened.

For many up-and-coming business moguls, angels have effectively served as their "Daddy Warbucks." But sometimes I wonder if angels are being exploited less for the right reasons and more for the wrong reasons.

The right reasons are clear. Startups have little collateral, marginal credit histories, and often bring bigger ambition than track records to the bargaining table. Banks and venture capitalists are in no position to entertain these individuals and, if they do, create conditions far too onerous for most to bear. So it is the angel who steps in with vital seed capital, the lifeblood of a scrappy startup.

The wrong reasons angels are in demand are more disturbing.

Maybe the latest business plans are not passing muster in the established investment community and angels are more susceptible to marginal ideas. I have heard some of the most ridiculous business plans and ideas being floated at networking meetings, made ever the more outlandish by adding the "dot-com" suffix to the end of the company name. So rather than beat the bushes for new and more benevolent angels to fund their unfundable business ideas, I wish entrepreneurs would adapt the same three rules when creating new ideas that we all use in hiring employees.

1. **Can They Do the Job?** Will the business plan actually create unique value that someone really needs?
2. **Will They Do the Job?** Does the management team have the skill and fortitude to execute the idea after creating it?
3. **How Will They Do the Job?** Is the value proposition of the new business structured in a compelling way that makes its success plausible?

If business plans and the entrepreneurs behind them would follow these simple rules, there would not be a shortage of angels. Blaming the marketplace for the failure of a new product or business is the oldest excuse in the world. Perhaps these entrepreneurs should ask themselves this hard question. "If I become a millionaire and can serve as an angel to the next generation of entrepreneurs, would I invest in my own idea?" That answer might be tough to take.

Business failures often teach us more than business successes.

6

FIGHT BACK, "DE-COMMODITIZE" YOUR PRODUCT ONLINE

No matter how you view the Internet, one thing is for sure. If you sell or distribute a commodity, you simply can't ignore online competition. Certainly your customers aren't.

Everyone knows a marketplace or an auction site where you can get a great deal on consumer goods or business products. If your customers think you sell a commodity, you face a dilemma: If you go online, the Internet will eliminate any price advantage you enjoy. On the other hand, if you don't go online, your competitors and your customers will anyway.

Here's what you can do. For years you have said that because of your extra service, experience, and expertise, you don't sell a commodity. You can prove this online. Actually, the Internet does give you opportunity for differentiation, and here's how:

- When selling your product, offer information of value, explaining why your methods of doing business matter to the buyer, then link your product to this information.
- Use fear, uncertainty, and doubt (FUD) to caution buyers against switching to unknown, unproven or lowest price competitors.
- Price your service, delivery, and advice separately from your product. Offer service, warranty, installation, and delivery services on an additional, a la carte, basis.

- Recognize that most Internet marketplaces commoditize products to explain them efficiently. Avoid the services that give your product no chance for explanation.

The way to make your commodity products survive and thrive in a price-sensitive, online world is to do what you always have done. Differentiate yourself, charge for value and give your product and company the same respect you expect of your buyers.

> **Never buy anything from a company that doesn't use what it sells.**

7

CUSTOMER RELATIONSHIP MANAGEMENT SOFTWARE: FINALLY, THE RIGHT THING OR JUST ANOTHER THING?

In the early 1990s, contact management software was popular among sales people, who used it to keep organized. It spawned an industry known as sales force automation.

Around the same time, business leaders heard the cries of marketers demanding that customer data be extracted from accounting systems on the company's mainframe. That led to database marketing automation, which also enjoyed success.

Today, almost a decade later, most companies with very large customer bases, sales forces or complex integrated marketing programs have invested in automation. Smaller companies have been more cautious and less successful.

Now there's a new trend – sales, marketing, and customer service automation have converged into "suites" of formerly stand-alone products. These suites are marketed further up the organization to senior executives of middle-market companies instead of the traditional target of IS managers in Fortune 500 companies.

The reasons are twofold: Senior executives make these decisions in smaller firms; and hardware, software, database, and Internet technology suppliers need to convert the corporate middle market in order to maintain sales growth. This repositioning has also brought about some repackaging - defining these products more in terms of the benefits promised than the features offered. It's called customer relationship management software (CRM).

CRM is being marketed as the tool a firm needs to take a systematic approach to finding, keeping, and growing customers. But does it work?

Companies with less than $100 million in sales face automation choices that are more confusing and riskier than ever. Has the time for CRM come, and has it come for your company? Will this latest "hot thing" catch on or become obsolete? Did the last "hot thing," CRM is expected to replace work, help or pay back?

The answers are a lot less complicated than you may think. First, assess CRM on your own terms. Recently, I attended the DCI and Ziff Davis Customer Relationship Management Shows in Chicago and Atlanta. At both, I saw a dizzying array of products, services, and ideas.

Some looked crazy and others looked extremely practical. CRM technology is more advanced than the needs of most mid-sized (less than $100 million) businesses. Specifically, few organizations have the resources or needs to use the features and functionality of some of today's hottest products.

For example, if your firm doesn't have a 100+ outside sales force, or several integrated marketing campaigns, many products will be overkill. Many suppliers sell products by the seat or user. If a smaller company wants to equip its sales, marketing, and customer service groups, only 10 seats may be needed. This is not a profitable deal for many vendors.

CRM suppliers may be assuming that their prospects have clear goals, a long time to implement changes and ample in-house resources to help employees learn the latest thing. For the average $1 to $100 million company selling to other businesses, I urge extreme caution and suggest five steps for CRM success:

1. **Ensure you clearly understand and have developed a process for how your business best finds, keeps, and grows its customers.** If you don't, you will end up with an automated version of your company's status quo. Your best practices must guide the development of a CRM system.

2. **Make sure your existing customer data is useful and used to make decisions.** While new systems can use existing information more effectively, only users can create new information.
3. **Clearly outgrow your system (manual or legacy).** There is no penalty for waiting a little longer. Whatever you buy will become obsolete, too.
4. **Have your staff agree on what it needs to do and build a plan to accomplish it.** Then talk to a technology vendor or consultant. If you don't assess your needs, you are likely to buy what they are selling and not what you need to achieve your plan.
5. **Recognize technology is a means to your goal of growing customers and sales, not the other way around.**

CRM systems can integrate the functions, activities, tactics, and programs that comprise a firm's sales, marketing, and customer service departments. They are generally reliable and technically will perform.

Now, more than ever, it is the responsibility of the buyer's senior management to define what its process for finding, keeping, and growing customers is and assure that implementation goals are set and met. Your company's success depends on it.

If It doesn't work
manually, it won't work
when its automated.

PART 3

Focusing Your Business Efforts

1

IF YOUR COMPANY ISN'T GROWING, IT'S FALLING BEHIND

You have started, purchased, or built a business. It has survived the first year in spite of multiple threats to its survival. Your firm has created products, services, and value for your customers. Employees, vendors, and partners have come to rely on you, and your responsibility to them has grown. As a result, your business has turned a profit, and you have started to prosper.

Now, you think to yourself, I've grown the business enough and it's time to finally relax.

But not for too long. While you relax, your costs will grow, your competitors will gain, and your customers will demand more. In fact, by choosing to 'not grow' your company, you are weakening its position with every passing day.

What is growth, really?

Growth is an increase in your company's top and bottom lines. Specifically, growth comes from:

1. Increased sales;
2. Profits;
3. Acquisitions.

Obviously, every company needs to create, sell, produce, and profit. But all of these things are byproducts of growth. Start defining your company as a growth company and organize your critical activities into these four key areas:

1. **Your firm's best and highest use:** Continually examine your firm's best and highest use. This is your company's reason for existence. Understand what makes your company special to your customers — and then produce more of it.

2. **Increased business and additional customers:** Always seek more business and additional customers. When you do this, it confirms your role in the marketplace. Understand what turns a prospect into a buyer. Provide low-risk options for prospects to try your products or services. Learn what it takes to create stable, repetitive customers. Turn your customers into your best advocates and champions.

3. **Delivering the goods:** Deliver what you offer. Measure, assess, and improve all that your firm does to meet your customers' expectations, and do it often. How can your services help your customer's business grow? What part or parts of your business do your customers value most? Do your costs reflect your value? Which customers pay your overhead?

4. **Profit and grow:** Assess your people, activities, functions, and programs in terms of how they contribute to the firm's overall growth. Create initiatives that deepen employee commitment to growth — both their own and the organization's.

Business, industry, and commerce are all about growth. Growth is all that matters, and all your firm's activities should reflect this priority. Take risks. Learn from your mistakes. And remember: *Standing still is always the same... as falling behind.*

> **Companies either grow or they are sold.**

2

BUILD CONTEXT,
NOT JUST CONTENT

In spite of providing increasingly better quality and service, why do we see customers suddenly change their demands, and often their loyalty? One answer is that customers will move to suppliers who offer context in addition to content.

What is content and what is context?

Content is the expertise or knowledge implicit in your product or service. For example, content is the experience, reputation, and education offered by attorneys and consultants and the formulations, shipping, training, and usage sheets which chemical companies that provide.

Context is *how* you apply your content to fulfill your customers' needs. It is more than customization or consultative selling. Context demonstrates your empathy with the marketplace, and how your services provide a breakthrough solution. *If you can create a context that is based on your firm's best and highest use, others cannot match you.*

Examples include Michael Dell, who took traditional direct marketing methods to sell customized computers online. Another case is Hallmark, that created "Bosses Day" to introduce personal relationship products into the workplace.

Is your business content-dependent?

The Internet has been called the world's largest copy machine because it can turn content into a commodity. Even if your company's information is protected by a copyright, patent, or secrecy agreement, your information is only a copier, scanner or "send button" away from worldwide availability. Despite your attorney's valiant and costly efforts to the contrary, your secrets cannot be the sole source of your competitive advantage.

Three examples of content-dependent businesses are:

1. Product distributors whose suppliers are leapfrogging them to establish direct relationships with customers. Customer databases and years of relationship are no longer absolute barriers to competition.
2. Copycat web sites appearing overnight and challenging successful web marketers, eliminating any advantage of being 'first in,' or an incumbent player.
3. Professional services previously billed by the hour are now unbundled. Some have been brought in-house, and what is outsourced is negotiated down to a fixed price.

Three ways to offer context.

Here's the bottom line: If the success of your business rests on proprietary content, the power to control that information may be slipping away from you and into the hands of your customers and competitors. Here are three ways to build context around your content.

1. Provide local, personal or event-specific information, such as showing your customers how they can make money using your services on a particular holiday.
2. Recognize how your customers really use your products and create custom versions for them. Instructions, warranties, and pricing can all be customized to fit the context of the customer.
3. Distribute and market your products directly to decision makers, not leaders. As an example, the receptionist/secretary in the smaller firm usually buys goods and services for the whole company.

Providing context is a matter of survival. Appealing to your customers as the 'low cost supplier' as your single point of difference is out of the question. Even niche marketing alone won't do it.

Be more nimble and smarter than your competition, by applying your content in your customer's context. The old adage is so true: *People buy holes, not shovels!*

> Buyers resort to price when sellers stop showing them value.

3

THE DILEMMA OF FOCUSING ON PRODUCTS OR MARKETS

As soon as a business becomes successful, an age-old question is sure to surface: Should we focus on products and brands, or on markets and customer segments?

Here are some guidelines.

It is better to focus on products and brands when:
- Products are in the development stage and need attention to succeed;
- Standardizing what you make and sell will increase gross margins;
- Your business is contracting and overhead is to blame;
- Your sales efforts are not consultative and don't need to be.

It is better to focus on markets and customer segments when:
- Customizing what you offer to customers will grow markets and profits;
- There is clear opportunity to penetrate accounts by meeting more of their needs;
- Your sales efforts are focused on a few, identifiable market segments;
- These markets have real differences that can produce profits greater than the cost of customization.

While mature organizations often shift their focus every few years, a few critical questions are timeless. It is always important to objectively assess the costs and profits of your existing focus and what your marketplace is actually demanding. Often, there is opportunity for aligning your efforts with their needs.

> **If it were not for people, organizations would work so much better.**

4

SIX TIPS FOR SELLING MORE TO MBAs WHO ARE LEARNING THEIR BUSINESS

There is an old saying, "The only thing better than having an MBA is to hire one."

Whether or not you are an MBA, we have all seen many such stars rise and fall through a company's ranks. If there is one common criticism of MBAs, it is that they can rely too much on their analytical strengths to compensate for the intuition that comes from many years of on-the-job training.

The reasons MBAs often have fewer years in a given job are well known. They include the churning corporate ranks of the '90s, accelerated upward career mobility and substantial corporate downsizing.

A less well known consequence of the MBA's career movement can be felt by those who have to sell to an MBA newly vested with purchasing authority.

Are your sales reps calling on MBAs who have little personal experience in buying or using what you sell? Without the benefit of a long-term relationship and the trust earned over time, the sales process can be difficult for both parties.

Faced with uncertainty when making a decision, MBAs are likely to revert to their training and focus on reducing risk. The buyer is likely to focus on lowering short-term costs, and demanding quicker paybacks on an investment. Regardless of how well your reps are trained in consultative selling, or how you motivate them to add value and grow your business, this scenario is difficult.

Here are six tips for selling to MBAs:

1. Teach them the business and create dependence. MBAs are trained to know what they don't know and find someone who does. Fill that void for them.

2. Ensure that your reps are really selling what the prospect wants to buy. As trite as it sounds, many buyers continue to make purchasing decisions based on criteria unrelated to how they were sold. Make sure your reps are selling advice, not just the product or service.

3. Sell with integrity. Prove to the buyer that he or she doesn't have to outsmart you.

4. Create FUD (fear, uncertainty and doubt) where appropriate. Using examples that show the down side of buying on price, or for immediate payback, can be invaluable.

5. Define the total and strategic impact of making a purchase. Most buying decisions do not fully reflect the value and cost of delivering products and services at the right time and place. Focus on maximizing potential rather than saving cost.

6. Find common ground. Like all employees reporting to the leader, buyers and sellers share the same personal agendas of reducing risk, hitting objectives, and getting promoted. Regardless of levels of education or experience, your sales force already has this in common with their prospect and can certainly find common ground here.

If these tips prove helpful, maybe the old adage can change to "The only thing better than being an MBA is having one for a customer!"

> **The only difference between an average and a great sales person is more confidence.**

5

WHY CAN'T WE ALL JUST GET ALONG? MAKING MARKETING WORK BETTER IN A MANUFACTURING BUSINESS

W hen it comes to finding new markets or developing new products, many industrial firms have trouble.

Three reasons why marketing can become a manufacturer's misfit.

When it comes to opening up a new market or developing a new product, many manufacturers have real challenges supporting and integrating the marketing necessary to be successful.

Too often, resources devoted to forward-thinking programs and projects fail and are terminated in favor of an existing sales effort focused on serving existing customers and products. Here are three reasons:

1. Manufacturers thrive by directly investing in the means (e.g., capital equipment) that clearly meet the needs of existing customers who buy the firm's production.
2. The high breakeven point faced by many firms requires an emphasis on the current month's sales and profits.
3. Those who can efficiently run machines and close existing customers have much of the decision-making power in a manufacturing firm.

To create new markets and products requires a supportive environment, mind-set, and investment horizon.

How to create a successful marriage of marketing, product development and manufacturing:

Marketing and product development should:
- Be given access to needed resources, set expectations, and meet them.
- Ensure that Marketing has a permanent seat at the management table.
- Break down projects into pilot, alpha, and beta phases with clear "go or no-go" checkpoints.
- Assure that responsibility for success is both individual and collective throughout the company.
- "Manage" the involvement of the sales force. Their input and support are critical, but the sales department's agenda is often different than that of new product development. The sales force's priorities are usually a result of their how they are compensated and otherwise rewarded.

Manufacturing and general management should:
- Make bets on forward projects, hedge these bets and then let their marketing horses run.
- Invest in multiple projects over time knowing that all won't succeed or fail.
- Leverage company resources through contributions from vendors, customers, and strategic alliances.
- Manage to intermediate deadlines and market feedback, not to a final sales number.
- Divorce the process of developing new customers and products from the monthly challenge of hitting sales goals.

Recognize that the obstacles to finding new customers and growing new products and services may have nothing to do with marketing. Infrastructure, cost or other performance problems are likely to surface. Separate project show stoppers from company-wide problems. Each needs independent attention.

Like human relationships, the answer to building a successful marketing effort in a manufacturing environment is tolerance, shared goals and commitment.

> The more dominant a company's sales culture, the harder the transition from entrepreneurial to professional management.

6

SELF-REFLECTION: PRACTICING WHAT YOU PREACH

In the spring of 1997, I left corporate employment and started a traditional one-person consulting business. Motivated as much by fear as by purpose, I created a service around a specific process tailored to help business owners focus on their best ways to find, keep, and grow more customers.

I invested in basic promotional and technological tools and networked to find clients. Fortunately, I was successful and my business grew.

But at one point, business slowed because my sales funnel was too empty after two major client relationships ended. Embarrassingly, I had forgotten to keep practicing what I preach. Even worse, I saw that my previous efforts were antiquated, random, and disorganized. **It left me two choices: Stop growing, or rebuild.**

Much has changed since 1997. I'm now part of a new industry I call Entrepreneurs eXchanging and Providing Expertise through Relationships and Technology, or the EXPERT Industry for short.

Due to a number of factors–including corporate downsizing, the Internet, easy-to-use personal technology, the need for workers with specialized knowledge, and a general desire for more independence, control, and quality relationships–a new form of business has emerged.

More than just corporate refugees, we knowledge workers have a unique network and work style.

In Northeast Ohio alone, there are hundreds of individuals who are in the EXPERT business. Business owners are also part of the EXPERT Industry, as they seek scarce human resources, which could ultimately change their approach to business.

With that in mind, I set out to refocus my firm, much as I do for my clients. Twenty years in corporate America taught me that conventional sales, marketing, and customer service efforts often fail to really find, keep, and grow more customers.

Many executives are frustrated with the results of their investments and seek unconventional assistance. I was no different, and once I realized it, I was able to take the necessary steps to change my business approach.

First, I defined my best and most profitable use–what is it that I was good at. The answer required a bit of self-reflection, but it was right there in front of me: The ability to synthesize and refine complex problems and then help force the implementation of simple solutions.

That's useful for any business, because it's imperative to break down problems in order to develop ways to expand a customer base. Furthermore, the EXPERT Industry requires a unique set of skills, such as a high preference for independence and facts over administration, bureaucracy and politics.

Next, I defined my **target market**: Businesses that sell their expertise or market a customized product to other businesses. I recognized that the service those people needed was development of a clear focus and process to grow their company's top line.

Then, I distilled the **crucial intersection** of the three PACER circles into one concise statement that described what my business did: PACER Associates works with companies who need to focus on their best ways to find, keep, and grow more customers.

We work with businesses that sell their expertise or market a customized service to other businesses.

Finally, I set out to reconstruct my **sales funnel.** Regardless of the funnel stage, all my efforts were centered on building awareness and relationships, using technology wherever possible. This is something I remained true to, in spite of having too few prospects in the funnel.

I defined my suspects as any business that sells expertise or markets a customized product to other businesses. I marketed through articles, speeches, seminars, and my web site, targeting presidents or business owners who were familiar with me through someone they trust and, independently, read about or saw my work. I also produced a free e-mail newsletter for more than 600 subscribers, and set out to develop referrals through clients and others in the EXPERT Industry.

Interestingly enough, the best sources of referrals turned out to be those EXPERTs who went through the PACER Process. This led to another development – the PACER Referral Network – where business owners can register their businesses online. This exposes people to the PACER Process while they exchange free referrals with other EXPERTS.

The net result is that I reinvented my business and put safeguards into place to ensure I would continue to practice what I preach to clients. The experience taught me that regardless of the size of your company, using the PACER Process was an intensely investigative and personal experience that results in a deeper understanding of one's business, marketplace and customers.

And, I found that doing so in light of the emerging EXPERT Industry would certainly help almost any provider or buyer of business products and services. Having a carefully focused message and a stable process for finding, keeping, and growing more customers is the reward for the effort.

> **The definition of insanity is doing the same things again and again expecting different results.**

Andy has a web-based training program on this chapter.
To order this course, visit www.pacerassociates.com

7

PROFESSIONAL SERVICE FIRMS: MARKET THYSELF!

When it comes to growing their practices, professional service firms of attorneys, accountants, financial advisors, and consultants spend much time, effort, and money building their image. They have worked hard to develop their talents and, since clients usually retain individuals and not firms, this makes sense. The creation of an "aura" around individuals delivering expertise is critical and reinforces credibility.

Traditionally, professional service firms market their image mainly through promotional means. Typical promotional efforts include:

- Seminars and forums;
- Public relations;
- Image advertising.

The problem with these promotional efforts, however, is that many firms assume promotional activity is marketing. In fact, promotional activity can be a distraction from the real opportunities for growth.

Very often, the real answer to growth lies in the other parts of the marketing mix. This includes target marketing, product development, pricing, and distribution. But many professional service firms de-emphasize these areas because they are much more personal, and this can be hard to face.

Here are examples in each of the major areas:

Target Marketing - Service firms are grown through personal relationships with a few key clients, which over time become the firm's base of business. Targeting markets requires choosing clients by more objective means and perhaps replacing those who have become friends.

Product Development - In a service firm, the partners are the products. To address this area, partners' performance and activities must be assessed, packaged, and managed.

Pricing - Hourly billing fortifies the value of individuals and their degrees. The more degrees or certifications, (JD, CPA, CFA, MBA, CMC, etc.) a firm can feature, the more it can bill. But clients buy solutions to their problems, not hours of talent. Isn't the selling of hours more of a convenience for internal accounting?

Distribution - Should the actual work product always be delivered through human means? Should personal selling and marketing be done to prospects or to the intermediaries who influence them? Are referrals the real way to grow clients? And where does the Internet fit in?

Whether or not the marketing of professional services can be completely accomplished objectively is always a problem. After all, it is tough when the owner, the president, and the product are one and the same.

But professional services firms can lose perspective. It happens when:

- There is a perception that professional services cannot be marketed and sold in a quantifiable and measurable manner.
- The individual in charge of marketing is neither a partner nor or a degreed professional in the firm's line of work.
- Marketing decisions are made mostly for partners with the most tenure and billings.
- Partner differences impede marketing decisions.

So how can partners of a professional service firm build a market-driven organization?

Here are some key steps:
- Recognize that a firm's core competence must include marketing.
- Bring in outside objectivity. Competence in one's profession does not necessarily translate into marketing expertise.
- Remove any organizational barriers between marketing and the executive committee.
- Don't hold marketing decisions hostage to differences between partners.
- Understand that the Internet is changing the very core of how professional services are delivered and marketed. Determine your firm's Internet marketing strategy, not just its web site.
- Look at the firm's base of business in terms of all of the ingredients of the marketing mix, not just promotional activities.

Some providers of professional services are nostalgic for a time when excellence was measured by their own profession. Today, all of us need to focus on marketing our businesses in addition to marketing our professions.

If you can't change the people, change the people!

8

ADOPT AN ORPHAN PRODUCT OR SERVICE TO GROW YOUR BUSINESS

With so many companies focusing on fewer products, services, and customers, why not make a home for another company's cast-off? Here are five ways to grow your business using this strategy:

1. Ask your customers which products and services their suppliers are ignoring.
2. Take your accounts that no longer fit within your company's focus and sell them to other providers.
3. Sell your competitors the products and services you are better at delivering.
4. Partner with your customers to meet their customers' needs.
5. Work with your suppliers to meet the needs of their other customers.

Paul Simon sings, "One man's ceiling is another man's floor." Find treasure in the orphan products and services of other companies.

One man's ceiling is another man's floor.

9

FIVE QUESTIONS TO ANSWER BEFORE "PRODUCTIZING" YOUR PROFESSIONAL SERVICE

There comes a time in every professional services firm when the need for non-time-based income is compelling. This can result from:

- Not having sufficiently skilled staff to personally deliver what every client was promised.
- Desiring a standardized version of the service to serve less affluent or smaller clients.
- Recognizing what your firm traditionally has customized can be standardized.
- Facing competition from new, lower cost, and possibly Internet-based competitors.
- Sheer exhaustion or burnout of the firm's staff.

Many professional firms fail to recognize that selling products is an entirely different task from delivering services. Myriad operational, financial, and practical issues arise once the decision is made, but even before this, a firm needs to confront itself and understand the implications of "productizing" its best and highest use. Five key questions include:

1. When is the time to start standardizing?
2. What will it take?
3. What are the new key success factors needed for success?
4. What is a reasonable investment in time, effort, and money?
5. When are outside resources required?

In other words, a services firm should recognize that selling a product is more than just packaging its expertise. It usually means creating a new product, often sold to a market beyond the firm's existing core. Conventional marketing wisdom holds that taking a new product to a new market is as much as eight times riskier than taking an existing product to an existing market.

Given the risk, perhaps first streamlining the delivery and production of your firm's service is better. Delivering a customized service, produced through a standardized process, can be more effective for all.

> If kept waiting to meet a prospect, leave after fifteen minutes. If they reschedule, your meeting will be better, if they don't, it wasn't meant to be.

PART 4

Fixing Your Business

WHEN TO USE AN ADVISORY BOARD, A CONSULTANT OR BOTH TO HELP GROW YOUR BUSINESS

Recently, while attending a program focusing on corporate advisory boards, I was reminded that these boards–unlike boards of directors–have no formal power or fiduciary duties, but rather serve at the pleasure of the business owner. Still, if given clear direction, they can be invaluable in assisting a CEO grow his or her firm.

Advisory boards, according to one of the course leaders, are preferable to consultants, who cost more and are more biased.

Having more than just an academic interest in this debate, I began to wonder when is it appropriate to use a board of advisors, a consultant or both?

Using a Board of Advisors

If carefully recruited, a board of advisors can provide a CEO with unbiased knowledge, expertise, and feedback. Advisors seem to be best at evaluating and appraising the ideas or directions the owner is contemplating or finalizing. Most advisors are busy senior executives and modestly compensated to serve on a board. Accordingly, they are rarely able to fully contest or disprove the summary information they are given, which usually arrives on short notice.

Rather, they can react with wisdom, counsel, and "a second opinion" to a pre-developed idea or plan.

The real value of a board of advisors appears to resemble that of a focus group. Focus groups are used by marketing executives as a way to predict the behavior of their marketplace prior to a product launch or other major promotion.

Successful focus groups demonstrate three common characteristics:

1. They are used to react to new ideas, concepts, and approaches, but never to invent a new idea.
2. The effectiveness of a focus group is largely the function of how well the moderator has prepared an agenda and a discussion guide for running the meeting.
3. They consist of intelligent, outspoken, and knowledgeable participants who constructively complement each other's opinions and reactions.

If advisory boards resemble focus groups, then the burden is on the CEO or president to serve as the moderator. He must prepare all the analysis, invent the new ideas, and ensure that implementation and other tactical plans are in place for a good board to absorb and provide a response. And this is where a consultant can help.

Consultants are like employees. A good consultant can be invaluable to a company leader if a specific skill set is missing or over-stretched within the company. Consultants bring expertise and experience and are generally unbiased if they are not selling other products or over-extending their assignments. Accordingly, consultants can prepare all the analysis, invent the new ideas, and ensure that execution and other tactical plans are in place. Furthermore, in lieu of staff, consultants can develop information, create tactics, and even implement programs. Boards cannot and will not do a company's work.

Use an advisory board and consultants together for maximum results.

Many presidents use an advisory board meeting as a forum for their employees and consultants to present progress on key projects. This way a company leader can oversee the development, creation, and production of the critical work and then have an advisory board react and respond to the results.

So, when should an owner or CEO use a board of advisors or a consultant to help grow their business? It does not need to be an either/or decision. Rather, use a consultant to help you when you don't know what you don't know, or to create what you don't have. Then use a board of advisors for unbiased input when you know what you don't know.

> Treat your employees like your customers and your vendors like your employees.

2

IF A CUSTOMER ISN'T PROFITABLE, THEN SELLING MORE JUST LIKE THEM MAY NOT HELP! FOUR SIGNS YOUR GROSS MARGINS ARE TO BLAME

Quite often, decisions to sell to a given group of customers or prospects are made by analyzing the "S" of SG&A (Sales, General and Administrative) on a company's profit and loss statement. It's rare that the direct costs of creating a product or service are broken down by customer segment. Instead, a "go or no-go" decision is often determined solely on the project's cost of sales.

Unfortunately this implies that the direct cost of creating every customer's purchase is equal and fixed. In many cases the direct cost of producing a product or service can vary by marketplace, customer needs or usage. This hidden cost data may not be captured through traditional cost accounting practices.

To assure that your gross margins are maximized within different customer segments, it is critical to:

1. Account for the time it takes to create a product or service for key customer segments.
2. Distinguish between the cost of creating the first customer order versus repeating the process for ongoing reorders.
3. Understand the varying levels of direct overhead (or overtime) that are required by different market segments.

4. Identify the differences in returns or re-work among major customer groups. A close look in this area may generate a clear opportunity or problem area. If we accept the 80/20 rule as a sacrament of doing business, which pockets of your business are contributing and which are being subsidized?

> **Decide with your head, implement with your heart.**

3

VISUAL BASICS: IF NO ONE READS ANYMORE, WHY IS THERE MORE DIRECT MAIL THAN EVER?

With the Internet, the Postal Service, the fax machine, and electronic documents, even the most conscientious or inquisitive among us can be overwhelmed. Many of us are secretly (or not so secretly) giving up and just not reading all we should.

Certainly, *unsolicited direct mail* is the first to be tossed into the wastebasket. So why then is there more direct mail than ever?

Nobody ever mails anything twice that didn't pay for itself once. Direct marketers are trained to mail up to the point of financial breakeven, which occurs when the value from responses does not cover the cost of mailing additional pieces.

I don't accept this explanation alone. Given the explosive growth of e-mail and the Internet (with its substantial cost advantage), and the ever-increasing cost of "snail mail," there are great alternatives to "ink on paper." Direct mail should be declining in use as a marketing tactic. But it is not.

So why is direct mail still such a critical and successful tool for so many marketers?

First, because successful business marketers focus on the key components of direct marketing. They know that the greater the percentage of response, the more successful the mailing can be. Their choice of mailing list will determine some 40 percent of response, the offer they make another 40 percent, and the creative approach, the final 20 percent. Business marketers know they will achieve success if they make intelligent decisions and execute them effectively.

Second, the needs of the business-to-business sector are growing. The goals of finding, keeping, and growing customers are creating countless problems for which direct mail is the perfect solution. These include prospecting, lead qualification, closing, keep-sold, win-back, referral development, and customer satisfaction measurements. The flexibility of direct mail, from its creation to its measurability, continues to be a highly predictable and practical solution.

Third, industry advances continue to add new value to using direct mail. For example:

- The quality and specificity of lists, along with continually improving database software, allows for smarter targeting.
- The high dollar value of business products and services lets marketers make really valuable and compelling offers to prompt prospects into qualifying themselves.
- The ability of direct mail to generate awareness and build traffic for a company's web site is often more effective than using search engines.
- The creative use of impact, dimensional, oversized, and colorful mailings will always provoke attention.
- Our confidence and ability to work with the Postal Service, reliably execute better programs, and accurately track results is higher than ever.

The usage and applications of direct marketing in finding, keeping, and growing customers seem to be as broad and as pervasive as ever. So, if no one reads any more, how come we still get so much direct mail?

Because it works.

Without advertising how would we know?

4

A TOUGH DECISION —
KNOW WHEN TO SAY WHEN

It happens too often; you launch a new product, service, sales initiative or marketing program with the best of intentions and lots of fanfare. As soon as the kickoff is over, your eyes turn to results.

At first, sales trickle in and then the trickle becomes a drizzle. But that's where it stops. The downpour never comes. The program is neither a success nor a failure. Once again, the market response to a new initiative does not meet expectations, and these questions remain unanswered:

- Do we have the right product or service?
- Have we positioned it correctly?
- Are we packaging, promoting, and pricing it correctly?
- Do we have the right market?
- Are we selling it correctly?

Your staff will answer these questions as well as they can, but you, the owner or profit center manager, are left with the familiar dilemma. "Do I fish or cut bait? Should I invest more to find out if the initiative can be successful, or cut my losses now?"

Financial analysis can help only so much. Breakeven analysis and return on investment calculations are important tools, but the assumptions applied can kill you, because there is no historical data.

So it comes down to your judgment.

Here are five steps to evaluate any new product, service or program initiative:

1. Reconfirm the objectives and sales or marketing process of the initiative. Are they realistic? Many initiatives in business fail because expectations weren't set, agreed on, and met. Sales and marketing efforts often fail due to forecasts based on market ignorance or under-funding based on the need to limit risk. If the goal is finding, keeping or growing customers, clarify this. Or, if the goal is creating more leads, reorders or referrals, make it clear. Otherwise results are hard to predict or see.

2. Require the champion and the implementers of the initiative to demonstrate a model for required success. Too often, the visionary on your staff who developed the idea is not experienced in implementation or vice versa. In fact, it may not even be the same person. Demand a clear model for success.

3. Establish probabilities of success to ensure the initiative can be successful. This step is where judgment, intuition, and previous experience converge. Bring your team together and agree on the probability of expected results.

4. Set up a field "test-kitchen" to demonstrate the required success. Stack the deck in one of the following ways: Pick a great sales territory, simple product version or traditional sales tactic and test your initiative. If your initiative is not successful, let it go. Be ruthless in preventing "scope creep" of the test, and stay committed to seeing it through.

5. Pick a drop-dead date or event for your decision. At a certain point you will know when you need to make a decision. It may be a moment in time or a reaction by the marketplace.

Tests like this always force a decision. They should not take longer than two to three months and frankly, in Internet time, can occur much quicker. The burden of the questionable initiative is that it saps the financial and human resources of an organization. It creates dissension and finger pointing within a company. Sometimes it may even be preferable to cancel a promising initiative than to let it linger. Often the idea is not the problem, it's just not right for a given organization at a given time.

5

IS YOUR CONSULTANT ACCOUNTABLE, OBJECTIVE, AND SHOOTING STRAIGHT? FIVE HARD QUESTIONS TO ASK

Consultants are often accused of regurgitating existing company knowledge and then providing top management with only the news they want to hear. While this occurs often enough to make most jokes about consultants both true and funny, what is a consultant's ultimate duty to:

- Tell the truth?
- Deliver unpleasant news?
- Be accountable for results?
- Resign instead of going along for a lucrative but ineffective ride?

Superior clients know that the following questions are the right ones to ask and agree on with a consultant. Do you want the consultant to serve you or the company? When does objectivity become intolerable?

1. Are you taking his or her advice?
2. Is too much of his or her income derived from your account?
3. Is the same consultant who previously recommended a program now responsible for providing or procuring goods or services required in the implementation phase?

4. Does your consultant receive a commission from the vendors he recommends to you?
5. Does he or she have a professional, emotional or financial stake in your firm's success?

There is growing concern over the issue of accountability in the largely unregulated consulting industry. Self-policing is always preferable and works best when its a two-way street. If we all ask and answer the right questions truthfully, everyone will be better off in the long run.

> For better and for worse, firing someone causes everyone else to feel his or her own mortality.

6

WHEN "IT HAPPENS": HOW TO FIX A FLAILING BUSINESS

Your customers are leaving you and possibly their customers as well, your costs are soaring and your long-term fixes won't work in time. What can you do when your company's back is up against the wall? Here is a quick plan:

1. Confirm your basic business strategy: Quickly decide on what is most likely to work and easiest to do.
2. Agree on available operating funds: Determine what you have to spend in the business.
3. Discuss which accounts and products you can service: Play lifeboat. Save only those accounts you can make money on now.
4. Determine three month objectives, activities, accountabilities for your surviving staff.
5. Discuss your decisions with your "keeper" staff.
6. Communicate your plan to banks, staff, customers and if necessary, the media.
7. Build a timetable and roll out strategy and stick to it.
8. Drive forward with this sense of urgency and it won't take long for your business to spring back!

As Jim Morrison sang, "I have been down so long that it looks like up to me!" Taking drastic steps in your business means you certainly won't make it worse!

> **Companies change only when the pain of change is less than the pain of staying the same.**

A LAST WORD ON GROWTH

In this book I have described some of the tactics and opportunities you can pursue to grow your business. With your focus and commitment, my suggestions will bring you results. But nothing will accelerate your success like bringing passion into your effort. For you, the owner, leader or entrepreneur, this should be easy. Your business is your baby! If you already have this passion, great! If not, you need to remember what you had when you joined or started the business.

As an entrepreneur or leader, you were driven to be successful. At first, survival was the name of the game. The fear of surviving kept you going through the next sale, payroll or quarterly statement. After a while, it did get better and easier. But now has it become too hard to grow your business?

To grow your business, you need to regain the same passion that got you started and apply it another way. This time, focus on thriving, not surviving. To do this means shifting your mindset from fear to confidence.

The is critical because fear keeps us alive but confidence brings us success.

We all know fear but what is confidence? I believe it is what drives our commitment. Based on our experience and practice, confidence gives us the ability to risk what we have and go for it! (And it is probably the best thing that grows with age!) As owners, we are all personally confident. The key is to reclaim our business confidence. When we have this, we can expand, commit and dedicate our organizations. We can take risky actions, often as much on instinct as on proof.

As our businesses grow, we should have more confidence and take bigger risks than those we took when we were smaller or on our own. But sometimes, we avoid change by:

- Fearing we could make things worse;
- Sensing we are powerless to improve it;
- Believing it is not worth the effort.

To break out of this trap I recommend you find a defining moment. (I had my own epiphany that you can read about next in the *About the Author* section.) What can be your defining moment? What positive or negative event can make you?

- Set different goals, dreams or expectations?
- Terminate failing programs, people, products or initiatives?
- Think out of the box, past the problem or toward the future?

Look for a defining moment in your business. It will give you the passion to become much more focused and disciplined. If you can't find a defining moment, create one!

I believe change occurs when the pain of change is less than the pain of staying the same. But often the risk of losing people, resources and time can hold us back. Should it? No. If properly valued, people and resources are always available. Only time is scarce. We always lose time in staying the same.

As owners and leaders, we have the most latitude to change our companies. So let's seize the moment and grow our businesses!

Here's to your growth.

Don't think, do it!

Andy Birol, President
PACER Associates, Inc.

www.pacerassociates.com

P.S. For a regular source of ideas on growth, subscribe to my free newsletter *Focus. Accomplish. Grow.* by going to www.pacerassociates.com

ABOUT THE AUTHOR

From the streets of Istanbul to Kenya's outback–
Cleveland's irreverent corporate change artist learned
his "survival" skills the hard way!

While many business leaders follow a more traditional path to success, Andy Birol has taken, as the Beatles coined, "the magical mystery tour." The "long and winding road" to success for this dynamic business development expert has taken him from the principal's office–where he landed after playing tag in the Blue Mosque in Istanbul–to the head of the class at Boston University, where he was awarded the school's highest honor for academics and leadership. The world has been the classroom of this energetic, results-driven entrepreneur. He has had stops in 45 countries and has seen most of the Seven Wonders of the World, celebrated a tribal wedding in the Kenyan outback, played soccer in the streets of Turkey and run races through the New York countryside. Along the way, he has also held jobs in just about every level of business. Now in his early 40s, Andy is an expert on the subject of business growth in the 21st century, and he uses his knowledge and expertise to help other business leaders grow their own businesses.

Raised in Istanbul, Turkey, Andy grew up during the Cold War. As a child, he watched the Russians bring their armaments down the Bosphorus Straits, while the U.S. 6th Fleet was docked near his home. He lived under martial law, when, on a bad day, people could have been killed for just stepping outside. With an American mother and a Turkish father, Andy found that he occasionally did not fit in as a child. He had no television growing up, so for entertainment, Andy would wake up at 4 a.m. to read his mother's issues of <u>Reader's Digest</u> before heading off to school. Spending his youth in Turkey gave him an important perspective on life and business in the United States. And when Andy was 12 years old and his family moved to Westchester County, New York, he was grateful to be living in this country. Says Andy, "I saw and really learned to appreciate, respect, and love what it meant to be an American. The American Dream became very real to me, for some reasons most people never get a chance to appreciate."

The American Dream for Andy has materialized in the form of PACER Associates, which he founded in 1997. This unique company employs the principles of the PACER process, a Process for Acquiring Customers and Enhancing Retention. The education he has received and the professional skills he has honed allow him to provide expert advice to business owners and top management personnel. Andy is also a prolific speaker, writer, stand-up trainer, and brainstormer. He uses his more than 20 years of successful business-to-business experience to deliver results for his clients. He's helped businesses from $1 million to $100 million in sales, including several Fortune 500 companies. He helped IBM produce leads that exceeded their goals by more than 100% and guided Actel Cellular as the company increased sales by more than 200%.

So where did Andy learn the tools of his exciting trade? Everywhere. His educational background and work experience are impeccable and far-reaching. He is well read, well traveled, and well versed in the dynamics of business. But his success and the success he helps others enjoy comes from the information and skills he has picked up by simply living his life. Andy is serious about business, but he is down-to-earth and often downright irreverent. He is bold, straightforward and uncompromising, but always ready with a joke. While other business consultants may illustrate their positions by alluding to passages in management books that most people have never heard of, Andy prefers to point to scenes in his favorite movies or popular television shows.

In fact, Andy says he is more like Hawkeye Pierce, Alan Alda's character in M*A*S*H than he is like his "stuffed shirt" counterparts. And he describes his job as being akin to the famous television series. Says Andy, "M*A*S*H was a chaotic situation where death was all over the place and the people saving lives dealt with it with humor. People forget to laugh in business and to connect with the 'other side' of business–the customers–from a compassionate perspective."

And when he describes how businesses should be run, Andy does not give credence to the cliché acumen "greed is good" of Michael Douglas' Gordon Gecko from Wall Street, but instead turns to the otherworldly characters of Star Wars. Says Andy, "I always think of the scene where they walk into the bar where it looks like feeding time at the zoo. The reality is that's what you're dealing with; businesses need to simplify it, codify it. The great thing about this scene is that everyone was there for a drink. The bartender there recognized that it didn't matter what these weird-looking creatures were doing; they wanted a drink–he served them, got paid and continued the process until closing."

In this galaxy, Andy's own path to business success has taken him many places, all of which gave him future inspiration. Although his family did not have a lot of money while he was growing up, they could fly anywhere they wanted because Andy's father, Mustafa, worked for Pan American Airlines, and Andy has traveled to 45 different countries throughout his life. Andy says his father's tenacity and work ethic had a big influence on his own desire to someday go into business. His mother, Jacqueline–who had been both a Broadway actress and a cover girl for a number of national fashion magazines–also passed on some valuable traits that would serve Andy well in his business endeavors. Says Andy, "Her intellect, acumen, and values complemented my father's attributes."

When Mustafa's international tour ended and the family moved to New York, Andy did not immediately adjust. The way of life in Istanbul was totally different from what he found in Westchester County. Says Andy, "This is 1971, the era of Vietnam and long hair and I have a crew cut." At first, Andy was doing poorly in school, and he had become a discipline problem. When he was in eighth grade and the track coach caught him throwing rocks and breaking school windows, Andy was ready to face his punishment. Instead, he faced a turning point. The coach asked him to try out for the cross-country team. Not only did Andy make the team, but he also became a marathon runner, was twice named to the all-county team, was chosen captain of the team, and broke a school record for the steeplechase. Says Andy, "It was one of the most significant early points in my life where I put in a lot of hard work and saw tangible results."

Andy has had jobs for as long as he can remember. When he was a kid, he set up carnivals and he managed six paper routes. When he moved to New York, he always worked at least two jobs, including stints as a lifeguard and pool manager. And when he was in high school, he added volunteerism to his schedule, spending time as a Big Brother to a boy who suffered from Muscular Dystrophy. After high school, he was accepted to Boston University as part of the school's early decision program. At that time, Andy already knew he wanted to study business.

During his first semester at Boston University, Andy's father suffered a heart attack and had to retire from his job, which meant there would not be enough money for Andy to continue his studies. But just in time, his hard work and tenacity paid off and Andy was awarded a scholarship by The Kemper Foundation that paid 50% of all his college expenses and gave him a job each summer with Kemper insurance companies. For three consecutive summers, Andy went to different parts of the country and worked in customer service support positions, and in sales and marketing. Andy says the experience laid some important groundwork for him. "This was the beginning of my education for working with companies as I do now," he says.

Andy graduated *summa cum laude* from Boston University and was awarded The Scarlet Key, the university's highest honor for academics and leadership. Higher education is important to Andy and his family. After his father's heart attack, his mother went back to school, earning three degrees, including a Master's in nursing administration from Columbia University. Upon his graduation, Andy deferred his admission to Northwestern University's Kellogg Graduate School of Management to work for Union Camp, a large paper products company. Andy characterizes his position with the company as "chief cook and bottle washer–doing all things sales and marketing for a senior executive." During his time at Union Camp, Andy accomplished the enormous feat of training 25 factories across the country in just 30 days. Before he enrolled in graduate school, Andy was promoted to New Project Planning, and he became the youngest manager in the corporation.

Andy received his MBA from Northwestern's Kellogg school in only 12 months as part of an accelerated four-quarter program. While many of his peers who graduated from the program headed off to Wall Street, Andy took an internship with the United States Association of International Development (USAID) and moved to Nairobi, Kenya. Andy's first assignment in Kenya was to help a wire and nail factory reduce material loss. Toting his Materials, Requirements and Planning (MRP) book, Andy planned to help the plant manager establish a system. When he got there, he discovered the wire was sent to the open-air facility once a year, and it was housed there during the country's six-month rainy season. So Andy put down his book and helped the plant manager build a roof.

Though violence broke out several times while he was in the country and he occasionally feared for his life, Andy has great memories of his time in Kenya. He and two of his USAID colleagues took a week-long trip through the outback, taking care to avoid warring tribes. Their driver was a member of the Kalenjin tribe, and during the trip, he had to stop off at a wedding. So he wasn't disowned, the tribesman had to dance a minimum of 12 hours at the wedding ceremony. Andy and his friends danced, too.

After his internship, Andy moved to Boston and joined Bank of Boston, where he developed relationship banking products while managing $2 billion of market deposits. Next, the New England Business Service of Groton, Mass., recruited Andy as Market Manager. There, he increased his profitability by reducing costs and increasing customer development, sales, and retention. Andy was very comfortable in Boston, but decided to move to Cleveland in 1993, when his wife, Joan, was offered a position here. Says Andy, "Moving was another formative experience for me because it taught me that if you feel a sense of futility, really change the rules."

Shortly after moving to Cleveland, Andy was recruited as Vice President of Sales and Marketing of a local company. Soon, he and Joan welcomed their daughter Margo, who was born with Cystic Fibrosis, an incurable disease. At work, Andy's business views were opposed to his employer's. At home, Margo was gravely ill and had to be hospitalized. Andy was soon confronted with another challenge. Says Andy, "The VP of Finance was my best friend and we had been at his house the weekend before with Margo hooked up to a tube. The CEO had this guy fire me. They all knew my daughter was very ill and I was sent out the door as if I was a common criminal. I went home and sat in my living room for a half hour before I had to go down to The Cleveland Clinic to see my daughter and said to myself, 'No one will ever, ever, ever, do this to me again.'"

Though she was just a small child, Andy looked to his daughter Margo for the inspiration he needed during that difficult time. Says Andy, "It was she who began to teach me what strength is really about. She made me focus on what is important and not important." So in the halls of Rainbow Babies and Children's Hospital, during Margo's three-week stay in 1997, PACER Associates was born. Through this exciting business, Andy is now teaching businesses to focus, just as Margo taught him. And Andy himself never stops learning. He has been selected as one of the few people to be mentored by Alan Weiss, the world's foremost authority on one-man band consulting. Andy is constantly refining his skills under Alan's auspices.

Andy took a chance by starting PACER, and now many businesses are reaping the rewards. Says Andy, "I had nothing except my tenacity, the talent I had gleaned from my experiences, my Rolodex, my ability to write and speak and to market the PACER process." Sandra Szuch, President of Inside Prospects in North Olmsted, Ohio, gives Andy much of the credit for her company's success. Says Sandra, "I wouldn't be where I am today without PACER Associates and Andy Birol. Our sales have doubled and my phone hasn't stopped ringing." Seth Harris, Marketing Manager of IBM Corporation of Waltham, Mass., agrees. Says Seth, "Andy's 'can-do' attitude and strong follow-through have produced leads exceeding our goals by over 100%. Everyone in the IBM Multimedia group was delighted with Andy's program for generating qualified leads."

Through his own life experiences, Andy has discovered how to help businesses survive and flourish. He teaches people to focus and to add humor to the workplace. He is dynamic, intelligent, and motivated. His expert advice helps business owners do what's best for their companies. In his own inimitable way, perhaps Andy puts it best. "I'm a consigliore to owners. I'm Robert Duval in The Godfather. Brando didn't do anything without Duval being involved in the decision."

PACER Associates is located at 5165 Ramblewood Court in Solon, Ohio. Their telephone number is (440) 349-1970. Their Web address is www.pacerassociates.com

CLIENT TESTIMONIALS

"Our relationship with Andy has been positive and worthwhile. He's more than a 'consultant,' he's a business coach. He's given us the confidence to go after business we'd previously shied away from. He's also a great sounding board, and someone we continue to share our success with."

Andy Zahuranec, *President*
WinPro Industries Inc.

"Andy did an absolutely wonderful job. He has the depth of experience to help his clients by understanding their business on a detailed level. PACER provided an exceptional value for us. I would highly recommend Andy Birol and PACER Associates."

Marilou Myrick, Founder,
President, and CEO
ProResource, Inc.

"Andy's strongest attribute is his persistence. He forced us to confront the realities of our business including where it was and where it should be. The result is a clear focus for the company, resulting in better production and an increase in sales."

Peter Calfee, *President*
Calfee Financial Advisors, Inc.

"I heartily endorse the PACER Process. It's the best way to develop a relationship with customers. Andy is extraordinarily perceptive. He easily identified issues that needed immediate attention."

Gary Bodnar, *President*
Actel Cellular

"Working with Andy Birol and PACER Associates was a highly-productive experience. Andy brought a process to organizing and completing our business development efforts."

Jeff Hanson, *Acting CEO*
ConnectSpace.com

"Andy is extremely knowledgeable and very helpful. Because of his wide and deep contribution in such a large number of areas, he is a virtual one-stop shop. I will continue to call on PACER and use Andy's help."

Mark Bogomolny, *President*
Landmark Products Corporation

"We've been successful, but we needed to move to the next level of sophistication in finding, keeping, and growing more customers. Andy brought process, structure, and new analytical thinking to our sales and marketing efforts. We now have better tracking and measurement of our sales and marketing tactics relating to our overall business goals."

John Finucane, *Managing Director*
Association Connections

"Andy helped us focus on assessing the success of a new product offering in a new market. He provided an independent view of real business problems with a clear focus. He always gave our business top priority."

John Milgram, *President*
Aexcel Corporation

"Andy's 'can do' attitude and strong follow-through have produced leads exceeding our goals. He produced enormously successful results and brought a well-orchestrated approach to growing our business. Frankly, he surprised everyone with what can be accomplished in business-to-business marketing."

Seth Harris, *Marketing Manager*
IBM Corporation

"As we prepare to deal with competition in the electric industry, Andy helped us to envision a new way to understand our customers better, what they are worth, and their strategic importance to the company."

Residential Market Strategy Team
FirstEnergy Corporation

"We hired Andy Birol to help increase Pease & Associates' marketing activities. As a result of his assessment of our firm and interviews with our clients, Andy helped us to become more focused than ever on growth. Through working with him, I became convinced to restructure my organization, reinforce my infrastructure, and drive my staff to meet higher expectations. Most importantly, Andy helped us to recognize our personal objectives and strengths and create a working environment designed to maximize growth. I am more enthusiastic about Pease and Associates than ever."

Joe Pease, *President*
Pease & Associates

"There are three outcomes when engaging an outside resource. 1) They tell you what you know. You don't need to pay an outsider for that. 2) They will tell you what they know without fully understanding your objective or challenges. Yes, you want their insights, but you want to know how they apply to your business, not a generic answer you can get from a book or an article in the Wall Street Journal. 3) The third outcome is what we sought and received from Andy Birol. He took the time to understand our business objective and actions we had previously tried to address it. He then shared examples of what other companies in similar situations did. Then we really got to work discussing the possible solutions. I will tell you there were times we didn't see eye to eye, and those were the conversations that enabled us to accomplish our objective: A systematic business to business selling system for our business."

Phil Yale, *Chief Development Officer*
ProForma, Inc.

CLIENT RESULTS

Actel Cellular, Cleveland, OH—As an authorized agent for AirTouch Cellular, Actel needed to focus on creating a sales program targeted at obtaining new business. PACER responded quickly; as a result, Actel enjoyed a 200% holiday sales increase, including 50% from inside sales.

> **Gary Bodnar,** *President*
> **Actel Cellular**

IBM Corporation, Waltham, MA—In need of a strategy for increased lead generation, IBM turned to PACER Associates. PACER developed an aggressive lead generation system for the Multimedia Group.

Andy's 'can do' attitude and strong follow-through have produced leads exceeding our goals. He produced enormously successful results and brought a well-orchestrated approach to growing our business. Frankly, he surprised everyone with what can be accomplished in business-to-business marketing.

> **Seth Harris,** *Marketing Manager*
> **IBM Corporation**

Inside Prospects, North Olmsted, OH—A developer/marketer of telephone-verified databases for Cleveland, Akron, and Canton. Inside Prospects needed an aggressive sales approach. PACER helped them double their business and create a profitable new service for its existing client base.

I wouldn't be where I am today without PACER Associates and Andy Birol. Our sales have doubled and my phone hasn't stopped ringing!

> **Sandra Szuch,** *President*
> **Inside Prospects**

NewMarket Solutions, Twinsburg, OH—An integrator of identification systems for schools, companies, and government, NMS needed to increase customer acquisition. PACER developed a process for identifying and qualifying prospects. As a result, NMS implemented the system, enjoying a substantial increase in new business.

Andy has a keen business insight. We've enjoyed a 26% increase in overall new business due to his recommendations regarding our telemarketing campaign. Thanks to Andy, we've found the single-most successful marketing campaign for new business, accounting for a 48% quarterly increase.

Jim Butcovic, *Partner*
NewMarket Solutions

WinPro Industries Inc., Mantua, OH—A custom manufacturer of high-end machined products, WinPro used the PACER Process to re-focus its business, implementing a successful system of lead generation and networking. As a result, new prospects were identified and sales goals were achieved.

With the help of Andy, our business has increased significantly. At his recommendation, we've developed a successful direct mail and telemarketing campaign directed at our target market.

Andy Zahuranec, *President*
WinPro Industries Inc.

Aexcel Corporation, Mentor, OH—A custom manufacturer of industrial paints and coatings, Aexcel needed to restructure their business plan.

Andy convinced us to shut off a costly drain on our results, which has been as critical as looking for new sources of revenue. Currently, he's in the process of developing a new direction and structure for a significant part of the company.

John Milgram, *President*
Aexcel Corporation

Association Connections, Oberlin, OH—An organization that provides discounts on freight for trade associations, Association Connections needed to grow to the next level. PACER provided them with a better system for tracking and measurement of sales.

Since working with Andy, we have instituted specific tracking efforts to justify and control our marketing investments. He has saved us many times his fee and has helped us to spend money more efficiently and effectively in order to grow our business.

> John Finucane, *Managing Director*
> Association Connections

ConnectSpace.com, Cleveland, OH—An Internet marketplace that builds on the tradition and fellowship of local business associations, ConnectSpace combines one-to-one business relationships with group buying and selling to help business owners network, sell more, spend less, and grow.

Andy helped build a focused and flexible Internet Business Strategy for ConnectSpace. He applied conventional business experience to a new medium in a most effective manner.

> Jeff Hanson, *Acting CEO*
> ConnectSpace.com

QUICK ORDER FORM

FAX ORDERS: (440) 349-0187
PHONE ORDERS: (440) 349-1970
E-MAIL ORDERS: abirol@pacerassociates.com
POSTAL ORDERS: PACER Associates, Inc.
5165 Ramblewood Ct., Solon, Ohio 44139-6015

Please send me _____ copies of *Focus. Accomplish. Grow.* @ $50

Please send me more information on:
☐ Consulting ☐ Speaking/Seminars ☐ Web-based Training
☐ Coaching   ☐ Expert Witness

Name _____

Title _____

Company _____

Address _____

City _____ State _____ Zip_____

Telephone_____

e-mail address _____

books _____ @ $50.00   Total _____

Sales Tax _____

Shipping _____

Amt. Enclosed _____

Sales Tax: Please add 7.00% for products shipped to Ohio address

Shipping by Air:
US: $10 for first book;
    $5 for each additional book.
International: $20 for first book;
    $10 for each additional book.

Payment:
Please send check or money order to:
PACER Associates, Inc.
5165 Ramblewood Court
Solon, Ohio 44139-6015

www.pacerassociates.com